The Blueprint for A House in Jannah

WAEL IBRAHIM

Transcribed and adapted from the lecture

"When The Gates of Jannah Open: Divine Promises for The Righteous"

Published by:

TERTIB PUBLISHING

Unit No. E-10-5, Jalan SS 15/4G, Subang Square,
47500 Subang Jaya, Selangor, Malaysia
+603-5612-2407 (office) / +6017-399-7411 (mobile)
info@tertib.press
www.tertib.press
@tertibpress (Facebook & Instagram)

Author	:	Wael Ibrahim
Transcriber & Editor	:	Nadiah Aslam
Proofreader	:	Arisha Mohd Affendy
		Hanis Husna Adzhar
Cover designer	:	Abdul Adzim Md Daim
Typesetter	:	Abdul Adzim Md Daim

THE BLUEPRINT FOR A HOUSE IN JANNAH

First Edition: December 2024

Perpustakaan Negara Malaysia

Cataloguing-in-Publication Data

A catalogue record for this book is available from
the National Library of Malaysia

ISBN: 978-967-2844-41-9 (hardback)

Contents

Preface 1

Introduction 4

Part I: All About *Jannah* 6

Chapter 1: *Jannah* is Attainable 7

Chapter 2: *Jannah* the Unimaginable Destination 10

Chapter 3: *Jannah* the Expensive Prize 16

Chapter 4: *Jannah* Through the Mercy of Allah 19

Chapter 5: *Jannah* the Eternal Home 24

Part II: The Ultimate Blueprint for Building Our Homes in *Jannah* *28*

Chapter 6: Deeds that Build Our Homes in *Jannah* 29

Chapter 7: Words for *Jannah* 31

Chapter 8: Acts of Worship 38

Chapter 9: Sins to Abandon 48

Chapter 10: Controlling the *Nafs* and Desires 66

Chapter 11: Embracing What We Can Control 72

Ending Remarks 83

Checklist 89

Arabic Glossary 91

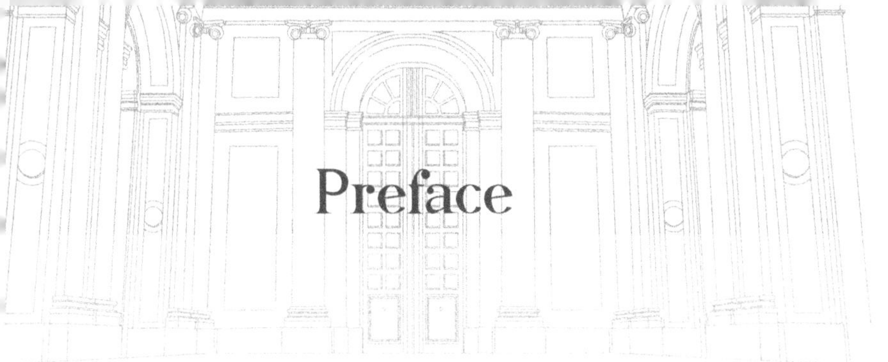

Preface

Assalamu 'alaikum, dear readers, brothers and sisters in Islam.

Welcome to a journey that is out of this world—literally! You are now holding in your hands a kind of manual to the most sought-after destination in the entire existence: *Jannah*. Now, I know what you're thinking: "Shaykh Wael, did you accidentally mix up your travel documents with your dreams for *Jannah*?" Rest assured, there isn't any mix-up. Let me explain this further.

In this book, we will explore the ultimate all-inclusive resort, where the facilities are endless, the stay is eternal, and the Owner is none other than Allah Himself, the most Generous and Kind. But unlike your typical vacation package, this one requires a bit more than just packing your bags and showing up at the gates.

Through these pages, we will unpack whatever we may try to conceive about *Jannah*—from its unimaginable beauty, to the VIP access granted only through Allah's mercy. We will dive into the blueprint for building our homes in Paradise—and trust me, it is a lot more exciting than any TV show you have ever watched!

But here is the catch: this is not just another "self-help" book promising you the keys to *Jannah*. It is a map about how to get there and what to expect when you are granted entry to the most awaited reward, the ultimate success, the success in this life and beyond. We will explore the deeds that lay the foundations, the words that raise the walls, and the acts of worship that furnish our eternal abodes. And yes, we will also talk about the renovations needed—those annoying sins we need to abandon and the desires we must control.

So, fasten your seatbelts (or tighten your *ihrams*) as we embark on this extraordinary expedition. Whether you are a seasoned traveller on the path to Paradise or just starting your journey, this book promises to excite you to live here in order to inherit there—*Jannah*.

Remember, in the race to *Jannah*, everyone is a winner—but only if they cross the finish line. So let us start this marathon with a smile on our faces and *taqwa* in our hearts. After all, Paradise is too beautiful to miss, and eternity is too long to be spent anywhere else!

May Allah make this book a means of guidance and inspiration for all of us on our journey towards *Jannah. Āmīn.*

Now, let's turn the page and start building our homes in Paradise, brick by blessed brick!

See you there, in *Jannah*, *inshā'Allāh.*

Wael Ibrahim

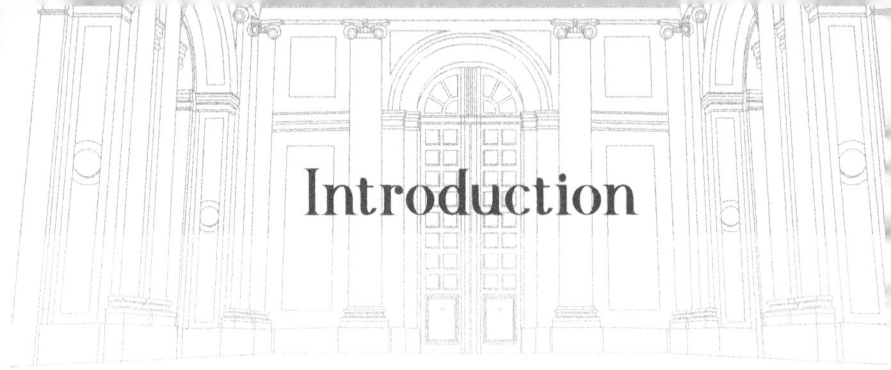

Introduction

Bismillāhirraḥmānirraḥīm

Assalamu ʿalaikum, my dear brothers and sisters.

Inshā'Allāh, I will be talking about "Building a House in *Jannah*" as a part of the book series "*When the Gates of Jannah Open.*" This book serves as a blueprint for building our palaces and houses in the eternal abode.

While flipping through the pages of this book, I would like you to write your notes about the knowledge you learn—the knowledge of Allah (s.w.t.) and the Prophet (s.a.w.). Why? Because when we write down the knowledge, it will *inshā'Allāh* retain in our minds. Consequently, we will be able to share and articulate the knowledge to the people around us.

Let us look closely at the incident of the first revelation regarding the importance of knowledge. *SubḥānAllāh*, as we look back at the first revelation, surah al-ʿAlaq, we can observe that Allah (s.w.t.) is commanding the Prophet (s.a.w.) through Jibril (a.s.) to read, "*Iqra'*," even though the Prophet (s.a.w.) was someone who was not able to read or write at that time. And so, the command "*Iqra'*" is not about reading literally, rather, it is about conveying the knowledge of Allah (s.w.t.) to the people as well as understanding the knowledge. Furthermore, within the same surah, Allah (s.w.t.) mentions the use of the pen:

ٱلَّذِى عَلَّمَ بِٱلْقَلَمِ ﴿٤﴾

Who taught by the pen

(Qur'an, al-ʿAlaq, 96:4)

The meaning behind the verse is that Allah (s.w.t.) is the one who taught us writing through the use of the pen. Why would Allah (s.w.t.) go to this length to mention the pen in the Qur'an? So that we will remember the knowledge. When we write down the knowledge we gain, when we pen down the *ʿilm* we learn, it is highly likely that we will remember it. Therefore, I hope that this sets the tone straight before we dive into the book.

PART I

All About *Jannah*

CHAPTER 1

Jannah is Attainable

What is Jannah all about?

Firstly, dear readers, we must understand that *Jannah* is only attainable through the mercy of Allah (s.w.t.) The Prophet (s.a.w.) mentioned in the hadith below that no one will be able to enter *Jannah* without the mercy of Allah (s.w.t.). The people, upon hearing this, asked the Prophet (s.a.w.), "Even you O' Messenger of Allah (s.w.t.)?" And the Prophet (s.a.w.) replied, "Yes, even me."

Abu Hurayrah reported Allah's Messenger (s.a.w.) as saying:

> None amongst you can get into Paradise by virtue of his deeds alone. They said: Allah's Messenger, not even you? Thereupon, he said: Not even I, but that Allah should wrap me in His Grace and Mercy.
>
> (Ṣaḥiḥ Muslim 2816f)

Thus, we should always ask Allah (s.w.t.) to bless us with His *raḥmah* and to forgive us for our shortcomings and sins—because we will keep falling back. We will keep making mistakes. We will keep making errors. Why? Because we are human beings. We are bound to make mistakes. However, the best of us are the ones who repent after making a mistake and try their best to improve themselves. Nevertheless, it is only through the mercy of Allah alone that we will be guaranteed the eternal bliss—*Jannah*.

Jannah is attainable through the mercy of Allah (s.w.t.)

CHAPTER 2

Jannah the Unimaginable Destination

When we say the word "*Jannah,*" bear in mind that this is the destination that surpasses all imaginations possible. Therefore, even though we try to visualise in our mind, it is something that is impossible to ever visualise. What we imagine is nothing compared to the beauty of the permanent abode of bliss. We cannot think of anything that is in existence which will be comparable to *Jannah* because it is a place that is beyond our imaginations. The Prophet Muḥammad (s.a.w.) mentioned in the following hadith as well that *Jannah* is a place where no eyes have ever seen, no ears have ever heard, and no mind has ever imagined:

Narrated Abu Hurayrah:

> The Prophet said, "Allah said, 'I have prepared for My pious worshippers such things as no eye has ever seen, no ear has ever heard of, and nobody has ever thought of. All that is reserved, besides which, all that you have seen, is nothing.'" Then he recited: "No soul knows what is kept hidden (in reserve) for them of joy as a reward for what they used to do." (32:17)
>
> (Ṣaḥiḥ al-Bukhari 4780)

Even the sounds in *Jannah* will be completely different. It is a realm that has never crossed any human's imagination.

In essence, whatever we think or imagine about *Jannah* is not *Jannah*. It is something that is just completely different from our imagination. However, that does not mean that we should not think or hope about what *Jannah* is like. Of course, it is not going to be the same as our imagination, but do immerse the mind in the imagination of the eternal abode.

I teach my children to do this as well. When my son was young, I asked him, "What do you want in *Jannah*?" He said, "I want to have a chocolate factory!"

That is definitely possible. I, on the other hand, want to drink a cappuccino in *Jannah*, and there is nothing wrong with me wanting to have that because it is possible. Allah (s.w.t.) is capable of doing anything and everything. So, would it be difficult for Allah (s.w.t.) to give me a cup of cappuccino? No, of course not. Allah (s.w.t.) is more than capable of doing that.

Moreover, the cappuccino in *Jannah* will not be the same as the one we have here in this *dunya*. That is why Mufti Menk named it "*Jannahcino*." In *Jannah*, the names will be different; the taste will be different. So do imagine living and enjoying the rewards of Allah in *Jannah*. There is nothing wrong with imagining it.

In fact, once, I was with my Shaykh in Hong Kong as he had come to visit. He was from the Middle East. *Alḥamdulillāh*, I was able to have a good time with him alongside my other friend as well. On the day my friend and I were dropping him at the airport, he had made a *du'a'* for us. My Shaykh said, "May Allah bless you and your family for treating me very well. And I hope that *inshā'Allāh*, when we get to *Jannah*, I want to invite you all to a BBQ meal underwater." This is what my Shaykh had said. I was puzzled, and I asked him, "Underwater? BBQ requires fire and coal, and water extinguishes fire. And we are human beings. So how can we breathe and eat underwater?" My Shaykh then recited the following verse:

لَهُم مَّا يَشَآءُونَ فِيهَا وَلَدَيْنَا مَزِيدٌ ﴿٣٥﴾

They will have whatever they wish therein, and with Us is more.

(Qur'an, Qaf, 50:35)

In *Jannah*, we will have whatever we wish for and even more so.

Can you imagine that?

Allah (s.w.t.) will give us more than what we wish for.

Back to my story. I then asked my friend what he wanted to do in *Jannah*. He said he wanted to fly. Afterwards, he asked me the same question as well. What came to my mind at that time was the story of the Battle of Badr and the story of Maryam (a.s.), Prophet 'Isa (a.s.) and the bird. I want to see these incidents right in front of me. That is one of the things that I want in *Jannah*. Of course, undeniably, the ultimate reward is looking at Allah (s.w.t.).

However, as I mentioned, it is not wrong to wish for other things as well. We can still wish for a cup of honey or a cup of milk or any other pleasures that we wish for because Allah (s.w.t.) is more than capable of providing them.

Jannah is a place
where **no eye** has
ever **seen**,
no ear has ever
heard,
and **no mind** has
ever **imagined**.

CHAPTER 3

Jannah the Expensive Prize

Jannah is not cheap.

Jannah is priceless.

The price for obtaining *Jannah* is not cheap. In fact, it is expensive.

How many of us hold a high position in society? For example, doctors, lawyers and so on. Most people do regard doctors as someone in a high position. Hence, I will be using this example.

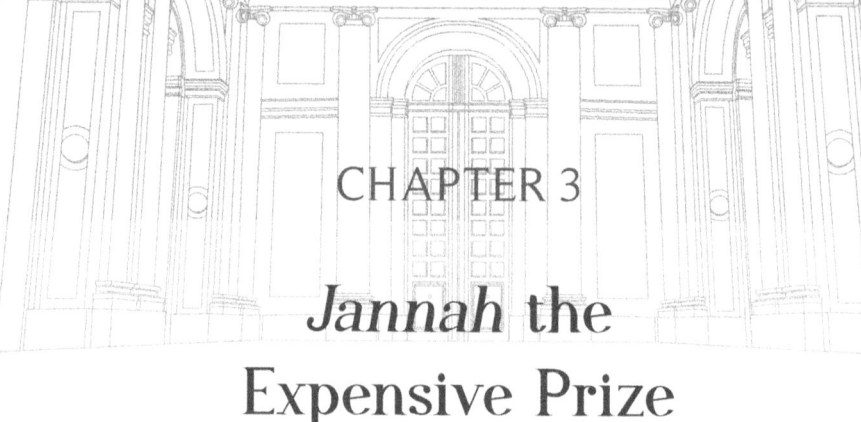

Do you know how long it takes for one to become a doctor? All in all, it is around ten to twelve years. Five years as an undergraduate, four years as a postgraduate and then a few more years of training to be a specialist. To achieve the goal of being a doctor, an abundance of thick books has to be read and studied. Additionally, a lot of time and hard work has to be poured in as well. In fact, the time and hard work spent are enormous.

Can you imagine the complications they have to go through? The sleepless nights and the huge amount of money spent just to study and become a doctor. It takes a lot to become one. This is only the reality of becoming a doctor, so why are we so laid back about *Jannah* as though *Jannah* is cheap?

Do you think *Jannah* is cheap?

Do you think *Jannah* does not require hard work?

If being a doctor is costly and requires an enormous amount of hard work, then what of *Jannah*?

In a nutshell, *Jannah* is not cheap. We need to work extremely hard for it. Some must be wondering about what I mentioned in the previous pages: that we can only enter *Jannah* by the mercy of Allah. Well, that explanation is for the next chapter.

Verily the
merchandise of Allah
is valuable.

Verily the
merchandise of Allah
is *Jannah*.

CHAPTER 4

Jannah Through the Mercy of Allah

Our good deeds, our good actions, and our hard work are signs of Allah's mercy.

When Allah (s.w.t.) has mercy on us to admit us to *Jannah*, He will guide us to do good actions. We are not entering *Jannah* through our good actions but rather through the mercy of Allah.

Do you understand this, my dear brothers and sisters? This is extremely important.

Our good deeds are a sign of Allah's mercy because He wants us to attain *Jannah*. Allah (s.w.t.) is giving us the opportunity to clarify the intention with ourselves that we are doing the deeds, because we do not want to just solely rely on Allah's mercy.

When we tell someone to quit smoking because it is haram, they will usually reply, "Don't judge me." The same thing happens when we try to advise and tell the sisters to wear their ḥijab properly. Some might advise people by saying, "We love you as our sister in Islam, but this is what Allah said." However, we receive a cold or defensive response.

Let me ask you a question, dear readers. Why do we kiss the black stone—*Ḥajarul-Aswad*? What do we do when we go to the Ka'bah? What do we do before the *ṭawaf*? We will go to the black stone, raise our hands and say "*Bismillāh, Allāhu Akbar*," and then kiss it. But why do we kiss the black stone? 'Umar al-Khaṭṭab (r.a.) once said while looking at the black stone, "I know you are a stone. You cannot harm me. You cannot benefit me. But had I not seen the Prophet (s.a.w.) kissing you, I would have never kissed you." Then he (r.a.) kissed the black stone.

Narrated 'Abis bin Rabi'ah:

> 'Umar came near the Black Stone and kissed it and said, "No doubt, I know that you are a stone and can neither benefit anyone nor harm anyone. Had I not seen Allah's

Messenger (s.a.w.) kissing you, I would not have kissed you."

(Ṣaḥiḥ al-Bukhari 1597)

The reason why we kiss the black stone is because it was an action done by the beloved Messenger of Allah (s.w.t.). The reason is basically for Allah's sake.

Let me give another example:

حُرِّمَتْ عَلَيْكُمُ ٱلْمَيْتَةُ وَٱلدَّمُ وَلَحْمُ ٱلْخِنزِيرِ... ﴿٣﴾

Prohibited to you are dead animals, blood, the flesh of swine...

(Qur'an, al-Ma'idah, 5:3)

Allah (s.w.t.) mentions in the verse that the swine is forbidden for us. The swine, blood and any dead meat are haram. Period.

Did Allah (s.w.t.) tell us why?

Did Allah (s.w.t.) give us the reason for it?

Some people say it is because of the worms that are found in the pigs, as they cause heart diseases and more. However, these discoveries were only brought to light at a later period—after the revelation of the verse. And so, is this the reason why we do not consume pork? NO.

The reason is because Allah (s.w.t.) said so.

We are the slaves of Allah. What do slaves do? They obey. They obey their Master, their Maker—Allah (s.w.t.). They say:

إِيَّاكَ نَعْبُدُ وَإِيَّاكَ نَسْتَعِينُ ٥

It is You we worship, and You we ask for help.

(Qur'an, al-Fatiḥah, 1:5)

This is what we say as the slaves of Allah: "To you alone Allah we enslave ourselves to." That is the *ʿibadah* we are required to do—to obey whatever He (s.w.t.) has commanded.

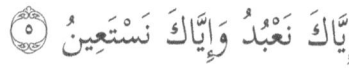

Our good deeds,
our good actions,
and our hard work
are signs of Allah's
mercy

CHAPTER 5

Jannah the Eternal Home

In this book, we will be building and looking through deeds that will help us build our homes in *Jannah*. While going through this book, I would like you, dear readers, to recite the *du'a's* and surahs as that is the purpose of this book: to build our eternal homes in *Jannah*. And so, make sure to recite them.

Do we know what the houses in *Jannah* look like? Similar to how *Jannah* itself cannot be imagined as it surpasses all imaginations—the houses in *Jannah* too cannot be fathomed.

The Prophet (s.a.w.) actually described to us how the palace-like homes in *Jannah* would look like. However, within the description, he (s.a.w.) used earthly language; meaning the words that we are familiar with, as that is the only way for us to understand *Jannah*. Imagine if there was a *Jannah* language, and all the hadith were in that language. We will not be able to understand a thing about the magnificent place called *Jannah* then. And so when we have no clue about it, then how will we be excited to go to *Jannah*?

Thus, in order for us to understand *Jannah*—what happens there, what kind of things there are, and more—the earthly language was used by the Prophet (s.a.w.). Do bear in mind that the similarity is only in terms, however, the essence of *Jannah* is completely different. Let me give an example. The Prophet (s.a.w.) mentioned in the following hadith that palaces and homes in *Jannah* are made out of gold and silver bricks and the ceilings are made of pearls:

Abu Hurayrah reported:

> I said, "What is Paradise built from?" The Messenger of Allah (s.a.w.), said, "Bricks of silver and gold, its mortar is musk of strong fragrance, its pebbles are pearls and rubies, and its soil is saffron. Whoever enters it will enjoy bliss without despair and eternity

> without death. Their clothes will not fade, nor will their youth expire."
>
> (Sunan at-Tirmidhi 2526)

SubḥānAllāh. Can we imagine ourselves living in that kind of house?

In essence, when we talk about building our homes here in this *dunya* and *Jannah*, it is completely different and beyond imagination. The palaces and houses in *Jannah* are something that can never be compared to and imagined.

Jannah is made of bricks of silver
and bricks of gold.
Its mortar is musk of a
strong fragrance,
and its pebbles are pearls
and rubies,
and its earth is saffron.
Whoever enters it shall live and
shall not suffer,
and shall feel joy and shall
not die,
nor shall their clothes wear out,
nor shall their youth come to an end.

PART II

The Ultimate Blueprint for Building Our Homes in *Jannah*

CHAPTER 6

Deeds that Build Our Homes in *Jannah*

Before we start building our houses in *Jannah*, we must first remember that not everyone is able and capable of doing some of the things—deeds. Some people can, and some perhaps cannot. Some people have the capacity and capability to do something others would not be able to do.

However, that does not mean that we should not try it, nor does it mean that there is no other way of building our homes in *Jannah*. There are, *alḥamdulillāh*, plenty of ways to create and build our palaces in *Jannah*. The important thing is that we have to find the ones that we are capable of doing. Additionally, *inshā'Allāh*, as we go through life, Allah will allow us to increase our capability of doing things as well. So, do not worry. Allah loves us, and He, too, wants us to be in *Jannah*.

In the following chapters, we will be building our houses in *Jannah* with a number of deeds. I have divided these chapters into five categories:

1. Things to **say**
2. Things to **do**
3. Things to **quit**
4. Things to **control**
5. Things that are **in control**

The reason why I am listing and breaking down these deeds into categories is so that I would like you, dear readers, to memorise, comprehend and use this knowledge well. May Allah bless all the knowledge that we receive.

Let us begin building our houses in *Jannah*.

CHAPTER 7

Words for *Jannah*

Let us begin our journey of building our houses in *Jannah* with the first category: things to say.

The Statement of Sincerity

The first deed that will help to build our houses in *Jannah inshā'Allāh*, requires us to recite surah al-Ikhlaṣ ten times—which *Alḥamdulillāh*, many of us have memorised. The Prophet (s.a.w.) touched upon this deed in the following hadith:

> Saʿid bin al-Musayyib reported in *mursal* form that the Prophet said, "If anyone recites ten times 'Say, He is God, One,' a palace will be built for him in paradise because of it; if

> anyone recites twenty times two palaces will be built for him in paradise because of it; and if anyone recites it thirty times three palaces will be built for him in paradise because of it." 'Umar al-Khaṭṭab said, "I swear by God, messenger of God, that we shall then produce many palaces for ourselves;" to which he replied, "God's abundant grace is even more comprehensive than that."
>
> (Mishkat al-Maṣabiḥ 2185)

Mashā'Allāh. Surah al-Ikhlaṣ is *alḥamdulillāh*, one of the surahs that the majority of Muslims know and have memorised. So *inshā'Allāh*, this action is something that we can do daily.

Therefore, dear readers, before proceeding to the next page, recite this beautiful surah ten times. In that way, *inshā'Allāh*, we would have built a house in *Jannah* for ourselves through the mercy of Allah (s.w.t.):

بِسْمِ ٱللَّهِ ٱلرَّحْمَٰنِ ٱلرَّحِيمِ

قُلْ هُوَ ٱللَّهُ أَحَدٌ ﴿١﴾ ٱللَّهُ ٱلصَّمَدُ ﴿٢﴾
لَمْ يَلِدْ وَلَمْ يُولَدْ ﴿٣﴾ وَلَمْ يَكُن لَّهُۥ
كُفُوًا أَحَدٌۢ ﴿٤﴾

Say, "He is Allah, [who is] One, Allah, the Eternal Refuge. He neither begets nor is born, Nor is there to Him any equivalent."

(Qur'an, al-Ikhlaṣ, 112:1-4)

(Recite x10)

Based on the statement of *aṣ-Ṣadiq al-'Amin,* the Truthful and Trustworthy—Muḥammad (s.a.w.), Allah has *inshā'Allāh* built a house for us in the eternal garden of bliss upon the completion of reciting the surah ten times. *SubḥānAllāh.*

Each and every one of us, including our children, has *inshā'Allāh* definitely memorised this surah. It takes only two to three minutes to recite the surah ten times. Therefore, keep this practice in our daily lives.

If we want more houses and palaces in *Jannah*, the trick is simple. We just have to keep reciting the surah.

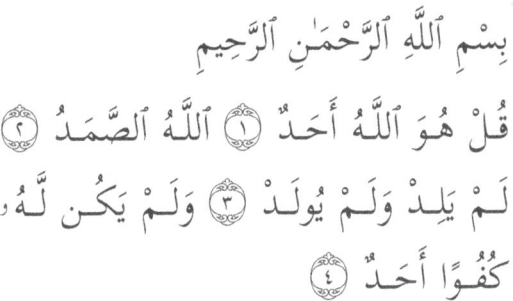

Du'a' Upon Entering the Marketplace

Salim bin 'Abdullah bin 'Umar narrated from his father, from his grandfather, that :

> The Messenger of Allah (s.a.w.) said: "Whoever enters the marketplace and says: 'There is none worthy of worship except Allah, Alone, without partner, to Him belongs the dominion, and to Him is all the praise, He gives life and causes death, He is Living and does not die, in His Hand is the good, and He has power over all things, (*Lā ilāha illallāh, waḥdahu lā sharīka lahu, lahul-mulku wa lahul-ḥamdu, yuḥyī wa yumītu, wa huwa ḥayyun lā yamūtu, biyadihil-khairu, wa huwa 'alā kulli shay'in qadīr*)' Allah shall record a million good deeds for him, wipe a million evil deeds away from him, and raise a million ranks for him."
>
> (Jami' at-Tirmidhi 3428)

The Prophet (s.a.w.) mentioned in the above hadith that upon entering the marketplace or shopping mall, if we recite the following *dhikr*, Allah will remove and extract one million of our evil actions and sins from our history. Additionally, Allah (s.w.t.) will also elevate our status in *Jannah* by a million degrees.

Therefore, recite the following supplication when we enter the shopping centre:

لاَ إِلَـهَ إِلاَّ اللَّـهُ وَحْـدَهُ لاَ شَـرِيكَ لَـهُ لَـهُ الْمُلْكُ وَلَـهُ الْحَمْدُ يُحْيِـي وَيُمِيـتُ وَهُـوَ حَـيٌّ لاَ يَمُـوتُ بِيَـدِهِ الْخَيْـرُ وَهُـوَ عَلَـى كُلِّ شَـيْءٍ قَدِيـرٌ

Lā ʾilāha ʾillallāh, waḥdahu lā sharīka lahu, lahul-mulku wa lahul-ḥamdu, yuḥyī wa yumītu, wa huwa ḥayyun lā yamūtu, biyadihil-khairu, wa huwa ʿalā kulli shayʾin qadīr

There is none worthy of worship except Allah, Alone, without partner, to Him belongs the dominion, and to Him is all the praise, He gives life and causes death, He is Living and does not die, in His Hand is the good, and He has power over all things.

(Jamiʿ at-Tirmidhi 3428)

It takes only ten seconds to recite this *duʿaʾ*. Thus, memorise it and recite it every time we enter the marketplace.

Do you know why we should read the supplication?

It is because we are entering a place that distracts us from Allah (s.w.t.). The marketplace or shopping mall is a *dunya* place which leads us to get distracted by the pleasures of worldly matters. It is the place where we forget about Allah (s.w.t.) and only remember about the *dunya* as we run after positions, status and materialistic items.

Thus, the Prophet (s.a.w.) is reminding us to be careful and not to forget Allah (s.w.t.) when we enter the hub of *dunya*-based attractions. Furthermore, by remembering Allah and reciting the *dhikr*, Allah will also reward us handsomely for it.

In essence, we must make that balance between the *dunya* and what is needed for our *akhirah*—hereafter.

Keep your tongue moist with the remembrance of Allah

CHAPTER 8

Acts of Worship

Let us explore the second category that will allow us to build our humble palaces in *Jannah*: things to do—acts of worship.

Praying 12 *rak'ah* of Sunnah Prayer

The Prophet (s.a.w.) mentioned in the following hadith that whoever prays twelve *rak'ah* of sunnah prayer per day and per night, Allah will build a house for them in *Jannah*:

Umm Ḥabibah narrated that Allah's Messenger (s.a.w.) said:

> "Whoever prays twelve *rak'ah* in a day and night, a house will be built from him in Paradise: Four *rak'ah* before *Ẓuhr*, two *rak'ah* after it, two *rak'ah* after *Maghrib*, two *rak'ah* after *'Isha'*, and two *rak'ah* before *Fajr* in the morning *ṣalah*."
>
> (Jami' at-Tirmidhi 415)

In the previous chapter, I touched upon the duration it will take for us to recite surah al-Ikhlaṣ ten times is two to three minutes. So, how about the two *rak'ah* of prayer before *Fajr*? How long does that take? It takes just a short amount of time, perhaps five minutes.

How about the supplementary prayer during *Ẓuhr*? Perhaps for some, the challenging sunnah prayer is the one during the time of *Ẓuhr* because of work. However, *wallāhi*, my dear brothers and sisters, when we sacrifice some of our lunchtimes for the sake of Allah, He (s.w.t.) will reward us immensely. Allah will replace that which we have sacrificed with something that is way better. Try this. Try replacing something for the sake of Allah (s.w.t.).

I did that, and *alḥamdulillāh*, Allah blessed me. I left music. Music used to be my entire life. It was my world, my addiction—it was in my blood. I used to live like that, and I was devastated. However, after leaving music and replacing it with time for the *deen*, *alḥamdulillāh*, things became different. Once, after I quit music, I was in an Arabic restaurant with my Shaykh. As we were sitting and eating there, the background music was playing, and it was quite loud. And so, because I had lived all of my younger days with music as my centre, I unconsciously started moving my head along with the music. My Shaykh then said to me, "Haram."

On a side note, sometimes, there are people who, without any explanation, will say "Haram." Please tell me the reason when you say that to me. Please give me an introduction of what I did wrong instead of scaring me. I remember when I went to the mosque to learn about the *deen* and Islam, I encountered some Egyptians there. And whilst we were talking, I laughed a bit too loud because we Egyptians get a bit too excited and loud when we meet each other. And so, I had laughed a bit too loud; I had raised my voice in an inappropriate manner because I did not know any better then. Suddenly, from the other end of the mosque, a man came up running while saying one word, "HARAM!" I tried to talk to the man, but he was unable to converse in the English language much. Instead, he started using his body language and hands—angry gestures—to explain that what I did was wrong.

The thing is, unfortunately, some people will always hunt us with the HARAM gun. They make it as if everything is haram and nothing is halal. No. My dear brothers and sisters, this is just not the case. *Wallāhi*, with everything that is haram in our existence, Allah (s.w.t.) has put in exchange thousands of halal alternatives. Remember this always.

Let me give a few examples. Allah (s.w.t.) has prohibited alcohol—one drink. How many drinks can we enjoy, halal-wise? An abundance. There are apple juice, orange juice, milk, tea, coffee and many more.

Allah (s.w.t.) prohibited one meat which is pork. How many other meats did Allah make halal for us? So many, *alḥamdulillāh*. Therefore, do not ever say that everything is haram because we are then making it difficult for ourselves and others. Do not be like the haram hunters. Do not block a discussion about wanting to know in depth what is haram and what is wrong with one's action; for instance, when the other party wants to know why their actions are deemed as haram and inappropriate.

In essence, do our best in praying these twelve *rak'ah* of sunnah prayer. Sacrifice some time for Allah. Sacrifice something for the sake of Allah. *Inshā'Allāh*, Allah will substitute it with something that is better.

Praying 4 *rak'ah* of *Ishraq*

The second action or act of worship we can do is to pray four *rak'ah* of *ishraq*—an optional prayer during sunrise.

What is *ishraq* prayer?

It is the prayer that we do after *Fajr*. After the sun has fully risen, we wait for about fifteen to twenty minutes and then pray two or four *rak'ah*. *Ishraq* prayer is also known as the special early *Ḍuḥa* prayer. The Prophet (s.a.w.) mentioned in a hadith that if we pray four *rak'ah* of *ishraq* before *Ẓuhr*, a house will be built for us in *Jannah*:

مَنْ صَلَّى الضُّحَى أَرْبَعًا، وَقَبْلَ الْأُولَى أَرْبَعًا بُنِيَ لَهُ بِهَا بَيْتٌ فِي الْجَنَّةِ

Whoever prays *Ḍuḥa* four *rak'ahs* and *qabliyah Ẓuhr* four *rak'ahs*, a house in heaven will be developed for him.

(al-Muʿjam al-Awsaṭ Lil-Ṭibrani 4753)

As we go through this list of building our humble homes in the eternal abode, I would like you to tick the boxes. I want you to tick the boxes of what actions you can do on a regular basis. At the end of this book, there is a checklist of all the deeds, so refer to it and tick the boxes. We do not have to do everything on the list, but it is best if we do.

This is because it is a bonus list; Allah (s.w.t.) is giving us the bonus, the reward of having a house in *Jannah* when we take the actions. So be busy building those houses, palaces, buildings and our road map towards *Jannah, inshā'Allāh*.

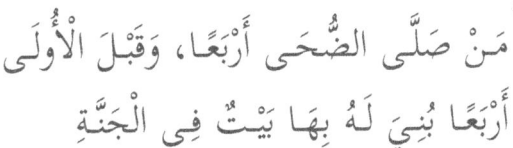

Building a Mosque for Allah

The Prophet (s.a.w.) mentioned in the hadith below that whoever builds a *masjid*—a place of worship—for the sake of Allah, Allah will build for him a house in *Jannah*:

> Maḥmud bin Labid reported that ʻUthman ibn ʻAffan decided to rebuild the mosque (of Allah's Apostle in Madinah), but the people did not like this idea, and they wished that it should be preserved in the same (old) form. Thereupon he (Hadrat ʻUthman) said:
>
> I heard Allah's Messenger (s.a.w.) as saying: He who builds a mosque for Allah, Allah would build for him (a house) in Paradise like it.
>
> (Ṣaḥiḥ Muslim 533d)

Some might say, "Oh, I'm off this list completely." "This action is just not for me." "I don't have the money for this deed." "I'm broke."

Dear brothers and sisters, I have interacted with a few scholars who have discussed this hadith. It is an undeniable truth that the majority of the people are unable to spend a large amount of money to build a mosque. However, if a few thousand people donate and give, for instance, $5, $20, $1,000 or however much to build the mosque collectively—Allah will *inshā'Allāh* build a house in *Jannah* for each one of the individuals. And so, do not ever belittle the amount we can donate and give for the sake of the *deen*, for the sake of Allah (s.w.t.). Do not ever belittle that.

Once upon a time, people thought that Islam would only be practised at Darul Arqam—a small house located in Makkah. Darul Arqam belonged to a companion named Abu 'Abdullah al-Arqam bin Abi al-Arqam. He was one of the early people to embrace Islam, and he allowed his house to be a place to practise and learn Islam. It was a small house that was hidden in Makkah as the people of Quraysh used to torture anyone who embraced Islam at that time.

That generation thought that Islam would only be practised there for life until 'Umar al-Khaṭṭab (r.a.) embraced Islam. When 'Umar (r.a.) embraced Islam, he initiated his conversion and the practice of Islam publicly. He publicly announced that he was a Muslim and that he would practise Islam without fear. *SubḥānAllāh*, because of that one man, Islam flourished. Why? Because he did not fear the people.

He did not care nor worry about what people would say about him. 'Umar (r.a.) told his family to embrace Islam as well, and if they did not, he would not speak to them.

In essence, initiate. Initiate doing these deeds for the *deen*. Initiate practising Islam. Do not be afraid to practise Islam in public. May Allah (s.w.t.) grant us the courage to live as Muslims and practise Islam without fear and without feeling the judgement of those who criticise us.

When we sacrifice something for the sake of Allah, He will replace that which we have sacrificed with something that is way better.

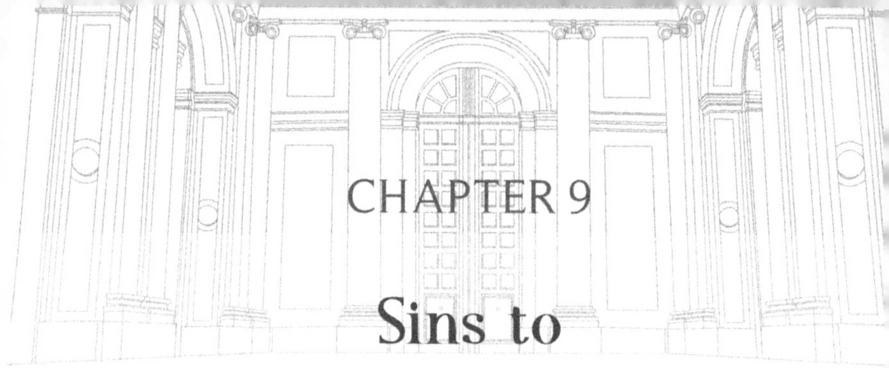

CHAPTER 9

Sins to Abandon

Let us explore the third category: things to quit. In this chapter, we will be discussing the hadith below in-depth:

> Narrated Abu Umamah:
>
> The Prophet (s.a.w.) said: I guarantee a house in the surroundings of Paradise for a man who avoids quarrelling even if he were in the right, a house in the middle of Paradise for a man who avoids lying even if he were joking, and a house in the upper part of Paradise for a man who made his character good.
>
> (Sunan Abi Dawud 4800)

Within this hadith, there are three houses that we

can build in *Jannah*: in the outskirts of *Jannah*, in the centre of *Jannah* and in the upper part of *Jannah*.

Quit Quarrelling

Narrated Abu Umamah:

> The Prophet (s.a.w.) said: **I guarantee a house in the surroundings of Paradise for a man who avoids quarrelling even if he were in the right,** a house in the middle of Paradise for a man who avoids lying even if he were joking, and a house in the upper part of Paradise for a man who made his character good.
>
> (Sunan Abi Dawud 4800)

The Prophet (s.a.w.) mentioned in the hadith that a house would be built on the outskirts of *Jannah* for the one who leaves an argument, even if they were right.

How many of us have had arguments that we have let off easily? How do we usually behave during arguments? When party A says, "Yes, you are right," to negate the tension, the other party would usually then reply, "Well, yes! I am definitely right." Do we behave like this? Unfortunately, we do. Sometimes, the argument might go like this: "You are wrong. You are always wrong." Sometimes, we end up fighting over the littlest of things, unfortunately.

What is usually the cause of an argument? Why do we argue? Why do we always want to prove ourselves to be right? Why do we want to prove that everyone else is wrong? Why? It is because of our ego and our pride; that is why we do not want to be proven wrong.

What is the punishment for having pride in our hearts? The Prophet (s.a.w.) said in the following hadith:

Is narrated on the authority of ʿAbdullah bin Masʿud that the Messenger of Allah (s.a.w.) observed:

> He who has in his heart the weight of a mustard seed of pride shall not enter Paradise...
>
> (Ṣaḥiḥ Muslim 91a)

As mentioned in the above hadith, the one who has even an ounce of pride will not enter *Jannah*. Even an atom's weight of a mustard seed of arrogance in the heart will stop us from entering *Jannah*.

My dear readers, how many of us are not on good terms with some people? Sometimes, we try to make amends with someone who does not want to talk to us anymore. Sometimes, when we try to initiate reconciliation, we would, for instance, say, "Hey, let's forget about what had happened. I love you for the sake of Allah. So, let's be on good terms again." However, the response that we receive in return is, "Hmph."

Have you experienced this before? I know a lot of people have. I know a lot of people would resonate with this matter. Unfortunately, every so often, the response we receive is, "NO! Don't talk to me. I will never rest until I see you burning in hell."

Some people will never forgive, and some people cannot forgive. I do understand that, at times, forgiveness is also misunderstood. To some, forgiveness means that we should get back together as to how things were before and let the past be in the past. That is not forgiveness. Forgiveness is usually related to the hereafter—not here, not the *dunya.*

The Prophet (s.a.w.) never allowed Waḥshi ibn Ḥarb to sit with him after he became a Muslim. Do you know who Waḥshi ibn Ḥarb is?

He was the man who killed the Prophet's (s.a.w.) uncle. He was the man who brutally killed Ḥamzah ibn ʿAbdul Muṭalib (r.a.) in the Battle of Uḥud. That same man who viciously killed Ḥamzah (r.a.) repented and embraced Islam. The Prophet (s.a.w.) mentioned in the hadith below that whoever embraces Islam, their sins of the past will be wiped out of existence. Allah (s.w.t.) would forgive all of their sins—no matter how big or ugly they are—as long as they embrace Islam sincerely:

> Narrated Abu Saʿid Al Khudri:
>
> Allah's Messenger (s.a.w.) said, "If a person embraces Islam sincerely, then Allah shall forgive all his past sins, and after that starts the settlement of accounts, the reward of his good deeds will be ten times to seven hundred times for each good deed and one evil deed will be recorded as it is unless Allah forgives it."
>
> (Ṣaḥiḥ al-Bukhari 41)

However, the Prophet (s.a.w.), too, is just a human being like the rest of us. He (s.a.w.) is also a human being with emotions.

Every time the Prophet (s.a.w.) saw Waḥshi ibn Ḥarb, he (s.a.w.) would recall the brutal and vicious way his beloved uncle Ḥamzah (r.a.) was murdered.

The Prophet (s.a.w.) did forgive Waḥshi ibn Ḥarb, but he (s.a.w.) could not bring himself to see him. And so, the Prophet (s.a.w.) said to Waḥshi, "I forgive you, but please do not come before me. Please do not cross paths with me." The Prophet (s.a.w.) said that because the pain was too immense for him (s.a.w.).

Basically, there are options. We may let go, forgive and forget, as people say, however, for some people, this can be hard. Some people cannot forget the past as the wounds are deep and still there. So, what exactly is forgiveness? Forgiveness means that on the Day of Judgement, we will tell Allah, "Allah, I do not want this person to burn in hell because of me. I forgive them, and I let go of their punishment." That is forgiveness.

And so, those who are quarrelling, what are you waiting for? Take out your phone and message them. Send them the message. Even if they reply to us with a "Hmph" or "I don't want to talk to you," it is all right. Nonetheless, send the message even if they reject us. At least we have done our part, we have initiated it. The Prophet (s.a.w.) said in the following hadith that the one who greets the other first—to the one whom they have argued with—is the better one:

Narrated Abu Ayyub Al-Anṣari:

Allah's Messenger (s.a.w.) said, "It is not lawful for a man to desert his brother Muslim for more than three nights. (It is unlawful for them that) when they meet, one of them turns his face away from the other, and the other turns his face from the former, and the better of the two will be the one who greets the other first."

(Ṣaḥiḥ al-Bukhari 6077)

Additionally, the gates of *Jannah* are not open to those who have not reconciled and to those who hold a grudge against each other:

Abu Hurayrah (r.a.) said:

The Messenger of Allah (s.a.w.) said, "People's deeds are presented before Allah on Mondays and Thursdays, and then every slave (of Allah) is granted forgiveness (of minor sins) if he does not associate anything with Allah in worship. But the person in whose heart there is rancour against his brother will not be pardoned. With regard to them, it is said twice: 'Hold these two until they are reconciled.'"

(Riyaḍ aṣ-Ṣaliḥin 1593)

The best of us are the ones who initiate reconciliation. Therefore, be among the best, dear brothers and sisters and *inshā'Allāh*, the gates of Paradise will be wide open for us.

Quit Lying

Narrated Abu Umamah:

> The Prophet (s.a.w.) said: I guarantee a house in the surroundings of Paradise for a man who avoids quarrelling even if he were in the right, **a house in the middle of Paradise for a man who avoids lying even if he were joking,** and a house in the upper part of Paradise for a man who made his character good.
>
> (Sunan Abi Dawud 4800)

Let us look at the second action that we need to quit to obtain a house in the eternal bliss: lying.

As mentioned in the hadith above, a house is guaranteed in the centre of *Jannah* for the one who avoids false narratives—lies. Can you imagine having a house in the centre of *Jannah*—the most expensive place?

On a side note, we can observe from this hadith the usage of earthly language, the **centre** of *Jannāh*. The terminology "centre" used by the Prophet (s.a.w.) here can be observed as a way for the Prophet (s.a.w.) to tell us that the centre is the best place in *Jannah*.

Back to the hadith: How many of us agree that lying is something that is absolutely common in our society? I am sure a lot of you are nodding your heads yes while reading this.

Unfortunately, this is the reality; this is the world that we live in now. It is now at a point where mobile phones, have made us liars as well. For instance, we have an appointment with our friends at 10 am. They call us at 10:30 am, wondering where we are as we are nowhere to be found. So, then they ask us, "Where are you?" What do we usually say then? "I'm stuck in traffic," even though the reality is that we just woke up and we have not even washed our faces yet.

I once had a similar encounter in Hong Kong about this. I was on the MTR train, and there was this man who was next to me, talking to his friend on the phone. He said to his friend, "You can't imagine the traffic I'm stuck in. I'll be there in a while." *Astagfirullāh*. I thought to myself, "*Wallāhi* brother, what traffic? We are on the train. What traffic is there when the train is moving perfectly well?" This man was speaking so loudly on the train that even the other passengers could hear him lying. *Astagfirullāh.*

Dear brothers and sisters, lying is the most hateful and ill-mannered thing in the sight of the Prophet (s.a.w.). A man once came to the Prophet (s.a.w.) and asked, "Can a Muslim be a coward? Can he be someone who does not have the courage to fight?" The Prophet (s.a.w.) said, "Yes. A Muslim may have that trait." The man asked another question, "Can a Muslim be a stingy person? Can he be someone who doesn't like to spend much?" He (s.a.w.) said, "Yes." The man asked another question. He asked, "Can a Muslim be a liar?" The Prophet (s.a.w.) said, "No." The Prophet (s.a.w.) said "NO" three times. That is how much the Prophet (s.a.w.) hated lying.

> Malik related to me that Ṣafwan ibn Sulaym said, "The Messenger of Allah (s.a.w.), was asked, 'Can the *mu'min* be a coward?' He said, 'Yes.' He was asked, 'Can the *mu'min* be a miser?' He said, 'Yes.' He was asked, 'Can the *mu'min* be a liar?' He said, 'No.'"
>
> (Muwaṭṭa' Malik Book 56, Hadith 19)

A Muslim cannot be a liar. In fact, there are only three situations where the Prophet (s.a.w.) has allowed "misinformation," not lies. In this context, it is not a lie, but it is misinformation. What are these three situations? The Prophet (s.a.w.) said in the following hadith:

Ḥumaid bin ʿAbd al-Raḥman bin ʿAuf reported that his mother Umm Kulthum, daughter of ʿUqbah bin Abu Muʿaiṭ, and she was one amongst the first emigrants who pledged allegiance to Allah's Apostle (s.a.w.), as saying that she heard Allah's Messenger (s.a.w.) as saying:

> A liar is not one who tries to bring reconciliation amongst people and speaks good (in order to avert dispute), or he conveys good. Ibn Shihab said he did not hear that exemption was granted in anything what the people speak as lie but in three cases: in battle, for bringing reconciliation amongst persons and the narration of the words of the husband to his wife, and the narration of the words of a wife to her husband (in a twisted form in order to bring reconciliation between them).
>
> (Ṣaḥiḥ Muslim 2605a)

1# Misinformation: During War

The first situation in which misinformation is allowed is during war. When we are on the battlefield, misleading our enemies is part of the battle tactics. Thus, it is not a lie but misinformation. We are trying to mislead our enemies so that they do not cause harm to our troops.

2# Misinformation: To Reconcile Two Parties

The second situation is when we are trying to reconcile two parties who are not on good terms. Let me give an example. There are two people who are not on good terms—Sister Fatimah and Sister Aisyah. And so Sister Khadijah goes to Sister Fatimah and tells her about what Sister Aisyah said about her, "Sister Aisyah was just telling me a while ago how you are the most beloved to her heart." However, dear readers, the reality is that Sister Aisyah said that she is the worst human being ever. And so, Sister Khadijah gives misinformation as she wants to melt the heart of Sister Fatimah and spark reconciliation between the two. Therefore, in this context, it is not a lie.

3# Misinformation: To Soothe the Hearts of Our Dear Spouses

The third situation is lying to your wife. Do not take this in the wrong context, dear readers, whereby *naʿudhubillāh* for the purpose of lying and cheating on her. No. This situation is not for when the husband is having an affair and tells his wife that he is busy at work. No. *Naʿudhubillāh*, it is not for that. I hope I have made this clear.

In this situation, lying to your wife means, for instance, complimenting her in the morning when she is in a bit of a messy state. Sometimes, the sisters like to put mascara and eyeliner on, but they do not remove them before they go to sleep. So what happens then? What happens in the morning? The mascara bleeds. The eyeliner and mascara have smudged their faces, and their hair is flying everywhere as well. And so, sometimes, when the husband sees that, they probably would want to say, "*Aʿūdhu billāhi minash-shaiṭānir-rajīm bismillāhirraḥmānirraḥīm.*"

So, instead of saying that, he can perhaps say, "You look different today," or, "You look beautiful today." He is a liar for saying that, but the intention is to please the wife by using nice words. However, do remember, dear brothers, to not exaggerate. Shaykh Husaini once said not to exaggerate the description. Otherwise, we will be called a big liar, and the wife would know as well, which consequently might hurt them. So be careful, dear brothers.

In a nutshell, do not lie. Abandon the act of lying. Quit lying, as it is a massive sin. In fact, the Prophet (s.a.w.) mentioned in the following hadith about the dangers of lying:

Narrated ʻAbdullah:

> The Prophet (s.a.w.) said, "Truthfulness leads to righteousness, and righteousness leads to Paradise. And a man keeps on telling the truth until he becomes a truthful person. Falsehood leads to *Al-Fajur* (i.e. wickedness, evil-doing), and *Al-Fajur* (wickedness) leads to the (Hell) Fire, and a man may keep on telling lies till he is written before Allah, a liar."
>
> (Ṣaḥiḥ al-Bukhari 6094)

Beware of lying because it will lead us to wickedness. When we constantly lie, we will then become a skilful liar. Nobody will be able to distinguish whether we are lying to telling the truth, and this will then be deception. Hence, be careful, dear readers, as lies lead to wickedness, and wickedness leads to Hellfire.

Quit Ill Manners

The third action that we should quit is ill manners. The Prophet (s.a.w.) mentioned in the hadith below that a house will be built in the upper part of *Jannah* for the one who makes their character good—who beautifies their manners:

> Narrated Abu Umamah:
>
> The Prophet (s.a.w.) said: I guarantee a house in the surroundings of Paradise for a man who avoids quarrelling even if he were in the right, a house in the middle of Paradise for a man who avoids lying even if he were joking, and **a house in the upper part of Paradise for a man who made his character good**.
>
> (Sunan Abi Dawud 4800)

How do we beautify our manners?

By quitting ill manners that are not in alignment with our religion—Islam. For example, abandoning the use of foul language. The use of the S word, F word and more has to be stopped at once. We have to quit the habit of saying those things. We have to erase and eradicate them from our dictionary.

Someone once asked me whether we could make a *du'a'* to curse the Zionists who are torturing our brothers and sisters in Palestine. He asked if we could use severe curse words. I said, "No," because we cannot alter those words, and once we say it, we cannot take it back. However, we can say the *du'a'* in a different manner, like, "Ya Allah, destroy these people and show us while we are alive a sign of your power for what they did against our brothers and sisters in Palestine."

We can pray against them without the use of foul language and then let Allah (s.w.t.) deal with them. When we use foul language because of some worthless people who have hurt our brothers and sisters, it is not worth the sin—it is not worth a dime. It is not worth anything. Thus, do not accumulate sins because of what they did and are doing. Instead, make *du'a'* against them. That is fine. Beautify our character. Be better than them.

May Allah protect us all. May Allah grant us entry to Masjid al-Aqṣa when it is in the hands of those who deserve it—the Palestinians *inshā'Allāh.*

Let them pardon and forgive.

Would you not love for Allah to forgive you?

Allah is Forgiving and Merciful

(Qur'an, an-Nur, 24:22)

CHAPTER 10

Controlling the *Nafs* and Desires

The fourth category that I will be talking about is things to control for us to obtain our homes in *Jannah*.

This is vital, so do pay heed, dear readers. The Prophet (s.a.w.) mentioned in the following hadith that, "Whoever guarantees the protection of their private parts, Allah (s.w.t.) will build for them a house in *Jannah* and will raise them in their ranks

Narrated Sahl bin Sa'd:

Allah's Messenger (s.a.w.) said, "Whoever can guarantee (the chastity of) what is between his two jaw-bones and what is between his two legs (i.e. his tongue and his private parts), I guarantee Paradise for him."

(Ṣaḥiḥ al-Bukhari 6474)

This is a grave matter as we are now talking about *zina*—adultery and illicit relationships. Some say, "We never touch each other. We just love each other."

Is this halal?

Is this permissible?

They say that they are just exchanging some "words" on the internet and social media and are not doing any touching or physical contact. Is this permissible? No. Do not joke with yourself. Do not kid yourself about this. It is haram.

Dear sisters, let me tell you something important. If the man does not move quickly to call your parents, then he is not serious about marrying you. Period. Even if he is someone who perhaps does not have the capacity or means to marry at the moment, he should still reach out to your parents and make clear his intention of marrying you one day.

To fool around behind our parents and do something haram on the internet is a form of *zina*.

The Prophet (s.a.w.) also mentioned in the following hadith about the *zina* of the eyes:

> Abu Hurayrah reported Allah's Messenger (s.a.w.) as saying. Allah fixed the very portion of adultery which a man will indulge in. There would be no escape from it. The adultery of the eye is the lustful look and the adultery of the ears is listening to voluptuous (song or talk) and the adultery of the tongue is licentious speech and the adultery of the hand is the lustful grip (embrace) and the adultery of the feet is to walk (to the place) where he intends to commit adultery and the heart yearns and desires which he may or may not put into effect.
>
> (Ṣaḥiḥ Muslim 2658a)

The eyes commit *zina*. The *zina* of the eyes is to stare at that which is not ours—at that which is not halal for us; to stare lustfully. Whether we look at haram images or videos on the internet or talk to non-*maḥrams* on the internet, it is still a form of *zina*.

Perhaps in the beginning, for instance, the sister wears her ḥijab properly—fully covered with no hair seen. She is a respectful sister who wears the ḥijab, *mashā'Allāh*. The brother, too, covers himself properly and often wears the *jubah* and brings his *miswak* everywhere with him. However, slowly into the relationship, things start to take a turn. What usually happens? The brother who used to cover up and wear *jubah* is now wearing a sleeveless shirt to show himself off. The *miswak* changes to a vape because it is apparently deemed cool. While the sister now has some of her hair showing out; she is now wearing more makeup, and then slowly, the ḥijab disappears. *Astagfirullāh*.

A lot of haram things are happening on the internet. Some people wonder and question me, "How do you know this Shaykh?" Well, I know because I have been counselling people for almost twenty-two years. Married couples are also affected by this, and they are miserable because of it.

A brother has a list of 1,000 sisters on his Facebook and Twitter accounts. He claims that they are just "friends," but that is not true. Unfortunately, this is happening on a daily basis. It is the most destructive thing as it shatters a household—a family, as the consequences of it are separation and divorce.

Infidelity is the most destructive thing that breaks a home. Infidelity is pernicious. Why does it come to this? Because we have let ourselves loose by interacting with the opposite gender; there are no boundaries and limits anymore as we have set it loose.

Some people do not mind shaking hands with the opposite gender. However, this is not allowed. When we advise people on this matter and tell them that it is haram, they will respond defensively and say, "Come on, Shaykh. This is nothing."

What did the Prophet (s.a.w.) say pertaining to this? He (s.a.w.) said:

> Maʿqil ibn Yasar reported: The Messenger of Allah (s.a.w.), said, "For a nail of iron to be driven in the head of one of you would be better for him than to touch a woman who is not lawful for him."
>
> (al-Muʿjam al-Kabir 16910)

It is better for us to be hit with an iron than to touch the opposite gender, which is not halal. So, keep this in mind, dear readers.

And do not come close to *zina*. Verily it is a great sin and an evil way.

(Qur'an, al-Isra', 17:32)

CHAPTER 11

Embracing What We Can Control

Let us dive into the fifth category, which is things that are in control; meaning things that happen to us without any power of our own. When something happens to us that is out of our control and power, it can be very painful. However, how we control ourselves during those times in terms of our words and actions to please Allah will allow us to be rewarded significantly.

The Prophet (s.a.w.) once mentioned that if we are hit with an ordeal or the calamity of losing our children, we should say, "*Innā lillāhi wa innā ilayhi rāji'ūn.*"

ٱلَّذِينَ إِذَآ أَصَٰبَتۡهُم مُّصِيبَةٞ قَالُوٓاْ إِنَّا لِلَّهِ وَإِنَّآ إِلَيۡهِ رَٰجِعُونَ ١٥٦

Who, when disaster strikes them, say, "Indeed we belong to Allah, and indeed to Him we will return."

(Qur'an, al-Baqarah, 2:156)

The Prophet (s.a.w.) discussed this in a hadith as well. When the angels take the soul of the child, Allah asks them, "Did you take the soul of My servant's child?" The angels will say, "Yes with Your command O'Allah." Allah then asks, "Did you take the soul of My servant's darling heart?" As we know, a child is the most precious being to a mother and father, hence, darling. The angels respond, "Yes." Allah then asks, "What did My servants say?" What did the parents say, dear readers? They said, "*Innā lillāhi wa innā ilayhi rāji'ūn.*" Allah then commands a house to be built for them in *Jannah* and named *Baitul-Ḥamd*—the house of praising Allah (s.w.t.).

Abu Musa Al-Ash'ari (r.a.) reported:

> The Messenger of Allah (s.a.w.) said, "When a slave's child dies, Allah the Most High asks His angels, 'Have you taken out the life of the child of My slave?' They reply in the affirmative. He then asks, 'Have you taken the fruit of his heart?' They reply in the affirmative. Thereupon He asks, 'What has My slave said?' They say: 'He has praised You and said: *Innā lillāhi wa innā ilayhi rāji'ūn* (We belong to Allah and to Him we shall be returned).' Allah says: 'Build a house for My slave in *Jannah* and name it as *Bait-ul-Ḥamd* (the House of Praise).'"
>
> (Riyaḍ aṣ-Ṣaliḥin 1395)

May Allah (s.w.t.) have mercy upon those who passed away among the believers, *āmīn*. May Allah (s.w.t.) ease the pain of those parents who have lost their children as well.

I sometimes visualise and imagine things. However, when this particular matter comes to mind, I try to reject it—I try to resist it. I cannot fathom losing my child. May Allah protect us all, and may Allah grant us the strength to say that which is pleasing to Him when we are struck with calamity. May we all remember to recite the *istirjaʿ*—"*Innā lillāhi wa innā ilayhi rājiʿūn*" during those challenging times.

I mentioned in my book *My Wheelchair* as well that the one *ayah* that woke me up and helped me get through the hardship was "*Innā lillāhi wa innā ilayhi rājiʿūn.*" What is the meaning of the verse? Indeed, we belong to Allah, and indeed, to Him, we will return. Our entire being, our entire body, our entire movement—everything that we think is our own is not ours; it belongs to Allah (s.w.t.).

So, why was I distressed when I lost my mobility? Why was I so sad? Allah has given me so many other things and blessings. Why was I so distressed about the one thing that Allah took away from me? If I do not belong to myself but to Allah (s.w.t.), then why was I so sad about not being able to walk? Only when I realised the true meaning of the verse and the embodiment of it did I start to get back to my senses, and *alḥamdulillāh*, slowly afterwards, I started to walk again. *Wallāhi*, only then I started to walk because I had finally realised. Before that, I was not focused on that part of my life and being belonging to Allah. Before that, I was stuck and despondent. I was stuck because I did not accept the *qaḍaʾ* of Allah (s.w.t.).

Many of us have gone through similar challenges—mentally, physically, emotionally, and psychologically. Some of us have been through the challenges of seeing the people around us pass away, for instance; family members, children, husbands, wives, parents, friends and so on.

I lost my father in the year 2011, and it was extremely painful. I remember training myself to say, "*Innā lillāhi wa innā ilayhi rāji'ūn*," as I was visualising his passing because he was sick and old. Hence, I was trying to prepare myself. I told myself to demonstrate patience and say what is pleasing to Allah when I hear the news—to utter "*Innālillahi wa innā ilayhi rāji'ūn*," when I receive the phone call of his passing.

Then the day came. It was at night, and as I was doing my work, I received a message from my sister. The message started with *innā lillāhi wa innā ilayhi rāji'ūn.* And then, she mentioned that our father had passed away. At that moment, I was so confused, and I threw my laptop. I did not know what to do. I was so shocked, and I was alone in Hong Kong at that time. It was just very shocking. Sometimes, we all get this kind of shock because we are all human beings.

There was once a lady who met the Prophet (s.a.w.)

at a graveyard. She was sitting by the grave, wailing and crying, and the Prophet (s.a.w.) was passing by her. He (s.a.w.) then said, "Be patient." The lady replied, "Get away from me. You don't know how I feel. It's none of your business." At that time, she did not realise the man was the Prophet Muḥammad (s.a.w.). People informed her about who the man was later, and they said, "How dare you speak like that to the Prophet (s.a.w.)!" The lady then went to the Prophet (s.a.w.) to apologise and said, "I'm sorry. Now, I am patient."

Narrated Anas bin Malik:

> The Prophet (s.a.w.) passed by a woman who was weeping beside a grave. He told her to fear Allah and be patient. She said to him, "Go away, for you have not been afflicted with a calamity like mine." And she did not recognise him. Then she was informed that he was the Prophet (s.a.w.). So she went to the house of the Prophet (s.a.w.) and there she did not find any guard. Then she said to him, "I did not recognise you." He said, "Verily, the patience is at the first stroke of a calamity."
>
> (Ṣaḥiḥ al-Bukhari 1283)

Ṣabr, patience is counted for us when we first hear the shocking matter—at the first stroke of grief.

In essence, we should say "*Innā lillāhi wa innā ilayhi rāji'ūn*" when we are struck with an ordeal and then sit and cry. Crying is a good thing. Do not let anyone tell us not to cry. We have all heard people telling us not to cry when we are already crying. However, the thing is, we are all human beings with emotions.

We do not have a button where we can swich ON and OFF our emotions. When my father passed away, some people told me not to be sad. I was in disbelief. Was I supposed to dance and be happy then? I was sad because I lost my loved one. One of the worst things for me is when people tell me not to be angry when I am already angry. What I need then is someone to hug me or someone to tell me, "*Inshā'Allāh*, everything will be all right. Let's do this together." I do not want someone to alter my emotions. I wanted to cry because my father passed away, my loved one passed away. That is all. It is as simple as that.

When the Prophet (s.a.w.) lost his son, Ibrahim, he was telling everyone that his eyes were shedding tears. He (s.a.w.) was crying. His (s.a.w.) heart was shattered. That was how the Prophet (s.a.w.) coped with the intense emotion of sadness. Tears are a sign of Allah's mercy.

The other key point of this incident is that he (s.a.w.) only said that which is pleasing to Allah (s.w.t.).

Narrated Anas bin Malik:

> We went with Allah's Messenger (s.a.w.) to the blacksmith Abu Saif, and he was the husband of the wet-nurse of Ibrahim (the son of the Prophet). Allah's Messenger (s.a.w.) took Ibrahim and kissed him and smelled him and later we entered Abu Saif's house and at that time Ibrahim was in his last breaths, and the eyes of Allah's Messenger (s.a.w.) started shedding tears. 'Abdur Raḥman bin 'Auf said, "O' Allah's Apostle, even you are weeping!" He said, "O' Ibn 'Auf**, this is mercy**." Then he wept more and said, "**The eyes are shedding tears and the heart is grieved, and we will not say except what pleases our Lord**, O' Ibrahim! Indeed we are grieved by your separation."

(Ṣaḥiḥ al-Bukhari 1303)

We are human beings. We are beings with emotions. However, there is one thing to keep in mind. The Prophet (s.a.w.) did something during his grieving, which we should all learn from. He (s.a.w.) said, "But we only say that which is pleasing to Allah (s.w.t.)."

In essence, we are entitled to our emotions. Allah (s.w.t.) created them for a reason, for us to feel them. Imagine if Allah created sadness, but we never felt it. It will then mean that Allah created something useless. What about happiness? Allah created happiness for us to feel it, not to push it aside; it was not for the purpose of not feeling it. So, if we feel happy, just be happy. On the other hand, if we feel sad, just be sad. Take in the emotions first. After a day or two, try to cope with it then.

Emotions are like waves. They are always changing based on the circumstances. However, some people tend to push away their emotions, and that is wrong. Therefore, dear readers, feel the emotions. If we are sad, cry and let it out; afterwards, stand back up again. If we see people crying, be supportive instead of telling them not to cry. Tell them to cry all they want. Tell them, "I'm here until you finish crying. I'm here with you." Additionally, do not apologise for our tears. Just cry all we want and afterwards things will change, *inshā'Allāh*. Keep reciting "*Innā lillāhi wa innā ilayhi rāji'ūn*" as well.

My dear brothers and sisters in Islam, we belong to Allah and to Him we shall return *inshā'Allāh*. So, why are we depressed over something that we have lost in the *dunya*? If Allah has promised us these beautiful homes and palaces in *Jannah*, then look forward to it and do our best to achieve it. How many rewards do we think we can accumulate if we were to recite surah al-Ikhlaṣ ten times every day until the day we meet Allah? *Inshā'Allāh* a lot. Just look at how merciful Allah is in rewarding and promising us these homes in *Jannah*.

Whatever you have
will end,
but what Allah has is
lasting.
And we will surely give
those who were patient
their reward
according to the best of
what they used to do.

(Qur'an, an-Naḥl, 16:96)

Ending Remarks

The topic that I have touched upon in this book requires us to achieve *qalbun salim*.

يَوْمَ لَا يَنفَعُ مَالٌ وَلَا بَنُونَ ﴿٨٨﴾ إِلَّا مَنْ
أَتَى ٱللَّهَ بِقَلْبٍ سَلِيمٍ ﴿٨٩﴾

The Day when there will not benefit [anyone] wealth or children But only one who comes to Allah with a sound heart.

(Qur'an, ash-Shu'ara', 26:88-89)

Now, the question is how do we get to *qalbun salim*—a sound and clean heart?

When I was young, my mother used to tell me to filter the rice. She would give me a big bowl of rice and then tell me to put water into the rice bowl; afterwards she would tell me to mix it with my hand and clean the rice. And so, I had to wash and remove the water a few times until the water and rice were super clean. That is not all. I must make sure not to make any mistakes of not checking for any black things and dirt. I had to make sure it was clean until my mother was satisfied, until the boss was satisfied; only then can we eat.

And so, this is exactly what we need to do for our hearts as well. We need to clean our hearts. We need to filter our hearts from anything that has even a tiny bit of *shirk*—anything that is classified as associating partners with Allah. For instance, believing in horoscopes and Zodiac signs; believing that, "I was born in May and based on my Zodiac sign reading, I will be lucky today." No. We must stop this at once. Once we believe in something other than Allah's *qadr*, it is *shirk*. We need to only believe that nothing can help or protect us other than Allah (s.w.t.) alone.

Back in the days, I used to have a starfish at my home. I would see the starfish before entering my house and I never understood what it was for. However, some believe it is for prosperity and good luck. In some other houses in Egypt, people would hang an onion at the entrance of their door. I asked my mother about it, and she said, "Because *shayṭan* does not enter a house that has an onion at its entrance." We used to believe that. I used to believe that. I used to believe that we were happy inside the house because *shayṭan* was outside, thanks to the onion. That is *shirk*. How can we believe that a mere onion can protect us from something as evil as the *jinn*? This is all rubbish. It is nonsense.

Therefore, filter our lives from *shirk*—filter our lives from sins. We must follow what is commanded of us; we must follow and do what is halal and leave and avoid what is haram. That is filtering. That is how we will be able to reach the level of purifying our hearts completely until we reach and meet Allah (s.w.t.) with a pure heart.

Additionally, the Prophet (s.a.w.) mentioned in the following hadith that there is a piece of flesh in our body, which, if it is sound, then everything else will be sound. However, if it is corrupted, then everything else will also be corrupted. This piece of flesh is the heart:

Nuʿman bin Bashir (r.a.) reported:

> I heard Allah's Messenger (s.a.w.) as having said this (and Nu'man) pointed towards his ears with his fingers): What is lawful is evident and what is unlawful is evident, and in between them are the things doubtful which many people do not know. So he who guards against doubtful things keeps his religion and honour blameless, and he who indulges in doubtful things indulges in fact in unlawful things, just as a shepherd who pastures his animals round a preserve will soon pasture them in it. Beware, every king has a preserve, and the things God has declared unlawful are His preserves. Beware, in the body there is a piece of flesh; if it is sound, the whole body is sound and if it is corrupt the whole body is corrupt, and hearken it is the heart.
>
> (Ṣaḥiḥ Muslim 1599a)

Inshā'Allāh, once we purify our hearts from *shirk* and sins, *bi-idhnillāh*, we will meet Allah (s.w.t.) with *qalbun salim*.

May Allah (s.w.t.) bless our brothers and sisters in Malaysia and all over the world.

May Allah (s.w.t.) grant our brothers and sisters in Palestine victory very soon.

May Allah (s.w.t.) make us rejoice when we hear about the victory of our brothers and sisters in Palestine, and may Allah (s.w.t.) martyr them.

May Allah (s.w.t.) take all of those who have passed away in the process into the highest level of Jannah.

May Allah (s.w.t.) reunite us with them in *Jannah al-Firdaws* with Prophet Muḥammad (s.a.w.) as well as with those who are honest and truthful, with the companions who accompanied the Prophet (s.a.w.) throughout the *ʿibadah*; throughout his message, *āmīn*.

Jazākallāh khayr. I love you all for the sake of Allah (s.w.t.).

In the body there is a piece of flesh; if it is sound, the whole body is sound and if it is corrupt the whole body is corrupt: it is the heart

Checklist

Have you done these deeds to earn your homes in *Jannah*?

Tick the boxes and start earning your homes in the eternal bliss—*Jannah*.

DAILY DEEDS	Mon	Tue	Wed	Thu	Fri	Sat	Sun
Recite surah al-Ikhlaṣ 10/20/30 times							
Pray 12 *rak'ah* of the sunnah prayer							
Pray 4 *rak'ah* of *ishraq* prayer							
Avoid quarrelling							
Avoid lying							
Avoid ill manners							
Protect ourselves from the haram							

OTHER DEEDS	Mon	Tue	Wed	Thu	Fri	Sat	Sun
Recite the *du'a'* before entering the marketplace							
Donate money to build a mosque							
Ṣabr and recite *istirja'* during hardships							

Arabic Glossary

Akhirah - Hereafter

Alḥamdulillāh - Praise be to Allah

Allāhu Akbar - Allah is the Greatest

aṣ-Ṣadiq al-'Amin - The Truthful and Trustworthy

Astagfirullāh - I seek forgiveness in Allah

Bi-idhnillāh - With the permission of Allah

Dhikr - Remembrance to Allah

Ḍuḥa - Morning supplementary prayer

Dunya - Worldly

Duʿa' - Supplication

Ḥajarul-Aswad - The black stone at the eastern corner of the Kaʿbah

ʿIbadah - Worship

ʿIlm - Knowledge

Inshā'Allāh - If Allah wills

Iqra' - Read

Ishraq - Sunrise

Jannah - Paradise

Jubah - A loose robe

Miswak - Teeth cleaning twig / a natural toothbrush

Muʾmin - Believer

Qaḍaʾ - Decree

Qalbun salim - Sound and pure heart

Raḥmah - Mercy

Ṣabr - Perseverance

Shayṭan - Satan

Shirk - Polytheism

SubḥānAllāh - Glory be to Allah

Ṭawaf- Circling the Kaʿbah

Naʿūdhubillāh - We seek refuge in Allah

Zina - Illicit relations

www.ingramcontent.com/pod-product-compliance
Lightning Source LLC
LaVergne TN
LVHW061344080526
838199LV00094B/7355
* 9 7 8 9 6 7 2 8 4 4 4 1 9 *